African American Men Struggle to Seek God

By

Melba Eldridge

© 1999, 2002 by Melba Eldridge.
All rights reserved.

No part of this book may be reproduced, stored in a retrieval system, or transmitted by any means, electronic, mechanical, photocopying, recording, or otherwise, without written permission from the author.

ISBN: 0-7596-8252-6 (e-book)
ISBN: 0-7596-8253-4 (Paperback)
ISBN: 1-4033-3747-0 (Dustjacket)

This book is printed on acid free paper.

1stBooks – rev. 11/1/02

Dear Veneda,

Delight yourself also in the Lord and He shall give you the desires of your heart !!!

PsAlms 37:4

Love ya,
Melba

3-23-03

Publications

Editor for research project: Regg Johnson

Editor for Adopted research: Dorothy Parker-Koger

Editor for book: Victoria Giraud

Photography: Charles Lee

Contents

Publications v
Photography: Charles Lee Contents.....................v
Contents...vi
Preface viii
Dedication xvii
Who will teach the children?...............................5

Photo: Who are your role models?....................13
Photo: Their search is for respect.....................21

Photo: Pride leads to destruction......................26

Photo: Is God's cost greater than His reward?.....33

Photo: Religious Imagery....................................41

Photo: Like father, like son. 53

Photo: Will she find the right man? 55

Photo: Three out of the four people in the congregation are women. 56

Photo: I am here for you now! 57

Original Research Paper..72
About the Author..80

Preface

African-American History class was one of three I needed before graduating in May of 1999. Being of African descent I was eager to take the class. An easy "A" I thought. I've been working with people for 20 years, why not take it? I should know a little about African-Americans by now. WRONG. That was the most strenuous class of the three.

If one were to attend church today, he or she would see that the majority in attendance are women. Getting to the root of the problem can help women understand the cause of the problem. There are a large number of people coming to church, but they are not staying in the church. This research paper can help one realize why some men refuse to come to church.

Why did I choose the subject: *African-American Men Struggle to Seek God*? I was scheduled to take a Bible Study class at church, but African-American History class fell on the same night.

Yes, I was very upset. No, I was furious. That is when I decided that if a paper has to be compiled, I will do it about church. I will teach them not to have a class on my Bible Study night. Why this subject? Why this title? The subject manifested while I was rehearsing for a play called "Removal of the Mask." The play presented scenarios of men and women, but mainly was concerned with boys and men. (Producer: Rev. Sediqya Pettaway) I played a wife with an abusive husband. The wife secretly attends church but the husband goes only on Christmas, Easter, Mother's Day, Father's Day and maybe for a funeral.

The producer chose me for the part because of my past. I too had an abusive husband who refused to go to church.

First and foremost, I praise God for the magnificent predestined journey of my life. There are many to whom I give thanks. My parents,

Taliaferro and Mae Eldridge; their Christian walk has led me accordingly. I thank God for them. My two sisters, Tanya Eldridge-White and Deborah M. Eldridge; I thank God for their support. My African-American History Professor, Patricia Rodney, who suggested publication of this research paper. Thank you — to God be the Glory.

I cannot write a book without a Publisher or Editor. Dorothy Parker Koger stimulated my interest through questions about my life. Regg Johnson: thanks for staying awake late hours checking grammatical errors on the original research paper. Charles Lee: I say thanks to you brother, for the Million Man March Photographs.

My children and grandchildren: what can I say? They are the BEST. Anthony A. Arrington and wife Bethany Ann with Alexis Ann and Josiah Joachim Arrington. Ayauna Arrington-Parker and her husband Donald Parker with Sydney Lenaye Parker. Anthony, Ayuana and I were in college at the same time, and we graduated one after the other. THANK YOU JESUS!!

My DESTINY is to stare life in its face and let God have His way in mine. I would like to play the Trumpet in Zion, which would be the beginning of the peace that passes all understanding.

To God Be the Glory.

African-American Men Struggle to Seek God is a compilation of information comprised from personal experiences and factual materials. This book stimulates one's thoughts and actions through pictures and/or Bible verses, highlighting specific areas of concern. It is also intriguing and very informative, providing an explanation as to why African-American Men struggle with religion.

Jennifer E. Martin

Hyattsville, Maryland

Oh sweet and heavenly Father, I thank you in the name of Jesus for your love and your saving grace. Lord, I thank you specifically for my sister, Melba Eldridge. Lord, I thank you for using her as a vessel to spread your good news of salvation and hope and for her willingness to be a laborer in your vineyard. Lord, you told us that your word will not come back empty; so I thank you now Lord for the brothers and sisters whose souls will be touched by this body of work. Lord, I thank you for allowing Sister Melba and each of us that have assisted her in this ministry to be a spiritual seed-planter and/or a spiritual seed-nurturer. Father, without you we can do nothing, but with you all things are possible. In the sweet, matchless name of your son Jesus I give all praise to you, God. Amen.

>Regg Johnson
>
>Silver Spring, Maryland

Dedication

To the loving memory of my Maternal Nurturing Grandmother: Annie M. Hargrove.

And to my Paternal Grandfather (Old Man River): Robert A. Eldridge, Sr.

African American Men Struggle to Seek God

What a wonderful God we have. He is the Father of our Lord Jesus Christ, the source of every mercy, and the one who so wonderfully comforts and strengthens us in our hardships and trials. And why does He do this? So that when others are troubled, needing our sympathy and encouragement, we can pass on to them this same help and comfort God has given us.

II Corinthians 1:3,4.

I hope this book will help someone who is troubled, needs sympathy and encouragement.

Melba Eldridge

African American Men Struggle to Seek God

Dear Heavenly Father, Abba, Jehovah, King, Master, the one who is and is to come; to the only true wise and living God, it is in the name of Jesus we come to you now. Thanking and praising you first for your continuous love of mankind.

Let this book we are about to digest be food for our spirit, soul and body. Let us not eat too much of this book per day, but savor each word until the desserts at the end.

Thank you for being an understanding God. Each situation might be different, but you still offer the same love, mercy and forgiveness today, yesterday and forever. Thank you!

Melba Eldridge

Please, Father, encourage the person who is reading this book to acquire a better understanding of themselves. Now unto Him who is able to do all things, hear the words of my mouth, and the meditation of my heart, let it be acceptable in thy sight, O Lord my strength and my redeemer. It is in Jesus name I pray. Amen.

African American Men Struggle to Seek God

Will this young child with the red hood remember the Million Man March, October 16, 1995, and what it stood for?

Who will teach the children?

Melba Eldridge

Train up a child in the way he/she should go, and when he/she is old, he/she will not depart from it. Proverbs 22:6 KJB

"In contemporary American culture, the religions are more and more treated as just passing beliefs — almost as fads, older, stuffier, less liberal versions, so called New Age — rather than as the fundamental upon which the devout build their lives." (Carter, 1993, p.14). This attitude is reflected in the African-American of the late Twentieth Century, who finds it harder to seek God. The struggle of African-American men seeking God may be due to their inhibitions, childhood trauma, pride, frustration, and/or false expectations.

One of the inhibitors, as stated above, of African-American men seeking God is childhood trauma. Childhood trauma is defined as "an emotional shock that causes lasting psychological damage." (*American Heritage Dictionary*, 1994). Some of this psychological damage is caused by the role models that African-American men choose. Often these role models are less-Godly men, versus Christian men, per Bernice King (1996, p. 93). This choice is made "because there are too few visible Black Christian men." (Ibid.) The only success for many young African-

American men — success as being defined by the world versus Christianity — is to become an athlete, a drug dealer, or an entertainer.

How many of us have seen others with nice families, nice clothes, and money in their pockets? Sometimes we wonder, "If there is a God, how come He didn't give me both parents, or money in my pocket and nice clothes? How come He took my Dad away? I'm a good person, I treat people nice, I thought God don't like UGLY. I ain't ugly."

I am reminded of a friend who watched his mother get beaten by a broom handle. Yes, it was by his role model, his dad. He said, "How could God let my Mother get beat down?" Then the trauma sets in; if he is my role model, then that means I should do the same thing, right? Like father, like son.

And he repeated the same actions as his father; he beat his wife for four and a half long years. So, what does love have to do with it? Should she stay because her children need a dad? Or should she stay because her education was limited, and she could not make a lot of money on her own? Till death do we part kept coming to her mind, and it almost was. What does God have to say?

Melba Eldridge

If we suffer, we shall also reign with Him.

II Timothy 2:12 KJB

Blessed are they who are persecuted for righteousness sake, for theirs is the kingdom of Heaven. Matthew 5:10 KJB

Melba Eldridge

African American Men Struggle to Seek God

Who are your role models?

When someone wants to do wrong, it is never God who is tempting Him, for God never wants to do wrong and never tempts anyone else to do it.
James 1:13 LB

Melba Eldridge

Some of the role models of young Black men provide conflicting messages, which add to the problem of young African-American men seeking God. Rev. Henry Lyons, a leader of the National Baptist Convention, for example, was viewed as a man of God; yet, on February 27, 1999, he was convicted of a crime against the Church (*Philadelphia Tribune*, 1999).

Everyone has faults, but God forgives and He loves you regardless of your past. A male friend of mine stated that, "If I submitted to an unseen God, I cry and admit that what I did was wrong, people would laugh at me. My friends would say, 'You stupid man!!' Then I can't drink liquor, smoke anything, or go out dancing NOWHERE!!! My friends would think I was PUNKING out on them. And give money to that PREACHER so he can get a limo. I don't think so. I've been to Church twice. They took up two offerings, and BEGGED for the third offering. You know, to make the pot even or something, they said."

A true friend is always loyal, and a brother is born to help in time of need.
Proverbs 17:17 TLB

Melba Eldridge

Who is out there; can anyone help this brother?

He is going to have children; who will help them?

African American Men Struggle to Seek God

There are friends who pretend to be friends, but there is a friend who sticks closer than a brother.

Proverbs 18:24 LB

Melba Eldridge

Behold, I stand at the door and knock; if any man/woman hears my voice and opens the door, I will come in to him/her, and sup with them, and he/she with me.

Revelation 3:20 KJB

African American Men Struggle to Seek God

The second inhibition for African-American men struggling to seek God is PRIDE. Pride is "a sense of one's proper dignity or value; self-respect." (*American Heritage Dictionary*). Pride's antithesis (the direct opposite of something) is submission, which is the ultimate requirement in seeking God (James 4:7). If an African-American man's pride was less valued, in a sense he would be in a better position to seek God. Seeking God gives an impression of weakness or vulnerability, according to Bernice King (King, p. 95, 96). Pride is also an inhibitor because some Black males see NO value in the Church. His values are based on how bad, tough, and macho he can be and how he can "drink his way to sobriety, steal his way to wealth, and lie his way to justice." (King, p. 19). His search is for respect. His respect is not found in the Church.

African American Men Struggle to Seek God

Their search is for respect.

Be with wise men and become wise. Be with evil men and become evil.

Proverbs 13:20

TLB

Which is your choice?

Melba Eldridge

African American Men Struggle to Seek God

I have heard some Black males say "That's my BOY, you da man, and keep it real, brother." Did they say that because in their past they cussed someone out, beat down people, drank you under the table, or even shot somebody for this respect? Is it always about who has the best game, the sweetest dunk, a stupid car, fine women or nice clothes?

I know someone who has it all and they are the Best. God!

Melba Eldridge

I put that ring on her finger, not God. I gave her that baby, not God. How come God didn't fix my truck when I needed it fixed? And if I do go to Church like SHE wants me to, where is my respect?

Melba Eldridge

Pride leads to destruction, and arrogance to downfall.
Proverbs 16:18

So be careful if you are thinking, "Oh, I would never behave like that." Let this be a warning to you. For you too may fall into sin.

I Corinthians 10:12 TLB

Melba Eldridge

There is a way, which seems right to a man and appears straight before him, but at the end of it are the ways of death.

Proverbs 14:12

African American Men Struggle to Seek God

"For by the grace (unmerited favor of God) given to me, I warn every one among you not to estimate and think of himself/herself more highly than he/she ought, not to have an exaggerated opinion of his/her own importance, but to rate his/her ability with sober judgment, each according to the degree of faith apportioned by God to him/her."

Romans 12:3 AMP

The third inhibition to seeking God is FRUSTRATION. Frustration is a process and that process consists of "Stress, which turns into pressure, and pressure into rage, and constant rage creates a state of weariness" (Jakes, p. 168). Some frustrations are caused by unemployment, little education, no money, bad relationships, etc.

The Black male is so focused on his stress that he fails to seek God. His focus is more on instant gratification than eternal salvation. This point is supported by John W. Thibaut's and Harold H. Kelley's Exchange Theory which states that:

"People evaluate relationships through a cost-reward analysis, weighing the energy, time and money invested against the satisfaction gained." (Thibaut, Kelley, p. 9-30).

The Exchange Theory explains that the cost is greater than the reward as far as time and energy spent. The energy spent leads to anxiety and frustration, which decreases the African-American male's emotional fulfillment.

Faith, or the lack of faith, adds to the frustration of the African-American man, which increases his inability to seek God. *Now faith is the substance of things hoped for and the evidence of things not seen.*

(Hebrews 11:1) KJB.

Melba Eldridge

Therefore, the Black male is seeking those things he can see (instant gratification) versus those things that he cannot see (God), which leads to the conclusion that he is not focused on seeking God, but on obtaining material riches.

African American Men Struggle to Seek God

Is God's cost greater than His reward?

Day by day the Lord observes the good deeds done by godly men, and gives them eternal rewards.

Psalms 37:18 TLB

Melba Eldridge

And you say, how I hated instruction and discipline, and my heart despised reproof!
Proverbs 5:12 AMP

I have heard some men say, "If I take a woman out to dinner, buy her stuff and flowers, I want her to put out too!! And I want her to love me like I want, not the way some book tells her to; I ain't with that."

"How am I going to get to Church? I don't have a car, and if I did I don't have any Church clothes. I could be looking for a job, but y'all want me to go to Church. When I do go, he (the preacher) just gonna tell me what I can and cannot do anyway. And I ain't ready to change either."

Cost and Reward

Melba Eldridge

If you then, evil as you are, know how to give good and advantageous gifts to your children, how much more will your father, who is in heaven (perfect as He is), give good and advantageous things to those who keep on asking Him!

Matthew 7:11 AMP

The last inhibitor, keeping African-American men from seeking God, is false expectations. Two false expectations are: racial issues and self-imposed religious requirements.

The major racial issue that inhibits the Black male from seeking God is religious imagery. Religious imagery is the image that one has of God and other spiritual beings. This point is supported by Na'im Akbar's quote in *Chains and Images of Psychological Slavery*.

"For African-Americans racial religious imagery is even more devastating. We have demonstrated that the one who sees himself in the Divine image is given an unnatural and a very inflated notion of what he or she is, which developed a kind of egotistical maniac. What is even worse, though, is what happens to the one who is not portrayed in the Divine imagery (the Black male), and who worships a non-self (the White male) in the image. In Judeo-Christian imagery, this means that the Caucasian bows down and worships himself, and the African-American male worships the Caucasian as a God as well." (Akbar, p. 52).

I have heard some Black males say, "How could Jesus be blond and blue-eyed if he lived in Africa where it is hot as Hell? His skin should be just as dark as mine if he ain't had no car and had to walk everywhere!"

This racial inhibitor combines with the lack of submission, as discussed in the above paragraph about pride, which further obstructs the African-American male from seeking God.

Melba Eldridge

Don't be bewildered or surprised when you go through the fiery trials ahead, for this is no strange, unusual thing that is going to happen to you. Instead, be really glad because these trials will make you partners with Christ in His suffering, and afterwards you will have the wonderful joy of sharing His glory in that coming day when it will be displayed.

I Peter 4:12,13 TLB

African American Men Struggle to Seek God

Religious Imagery

If I do go to Church, will the congregation respect me and my family?

Melba Eldridge

The extent and boldness of my sin involved almost all evil in the estimation of the congregation and community.

Proverbs 5:14 AMP

Melba Eldridge

The man who is not a Christian cannot understand and cannot accept these thoughts from God, which the Holy Spirit teaches us. They sound foolish to him, because only those who have the Holy Spirit within them can understand what the Holy Spirit means. Others just cannot take it in. But the spiritual man has insight into everything.

I Corinthians 2:14,15 LB

African American Men Struggle to Seek God

False Expectations

I can't go to Church like THIS!!!

Melba Eldridge

And why should you be anxious about clothes? Consider the lilies of the field and learn thoroughly how they grow; they neither toil nor spin; yet I tell you even Solomon in all his magnificence, excellence, dignity and grace was not arrayed like one of these. But God so clothes the grass of the field, which today is alive and green and tomorrow is tossed into the furnace. Will He not much more surely clothe you, O you men with little faith?

Matthew 6:28-30

The second false expectation, which inhibits African-American men from seeking God, is self-imposed religious requirements. These religious requirements are self-imposed because one places them upon oneself, but they have no religious basis. Examples of self-imposed religious requirements are: dress code (I must wear a suit, tie, dress shoes, comb my hair, etc.), a life devoid of entertainment (no more clubs, drinking, smoking whatever, sleeping with whoever), spiritual worthiness (there's no way God can forgive me for what I've done).

Other people's impression of self (he must have done something really bad if **he's** going to Church) and economic concerns (to make someone else happy). These and many other self-imposed requirements inhibit the African-American male from seeking God.

Four reasons why African-American males do not seek God are: childhood trauma, pride, frustration and false expectations. Although these inhibitors exist, there is still a need for African-American men to seek God. Religion is "the fundamental upon which the devout build their lives." (Carter, p. 14).

African American Men Struggle to Seek God

African-American males could reach their true potential if they seek God first, then everything else will be added unto them.

But seek for, aim at, and strive after first of all His kingdom, and His righteousness, His way of doing and being right, and then all these things taken together will be given you besides.

Matthew 6:33 AMP

Melba Eldridge

African-American women want the Black males to realize who they are and to be free to reach their full potential.

Do not be afraid and feel that if your dreams do not come true it's over. Learn to operate in trust with God; let Him be in control. Learn to love people — not try to own them. Give the Gift of freedom. If it is Love, it will come back to you, if it doesn't, it never was.

Isaiah 55:11

Melba Eldridge

God is love and He wants us to love each other.

I John 4:11,16

African American Men Struggle to Seek God

Like father, like son.

Should we go to Church? What do we have to lose but our souls?

Melba Eldridge

Delight yourself also in the Lord. And He will give you the desires and secret petitions of your heart.

Psalms 37:4 AMP

African American Men Struggle to Seek God

I cannot look at her.

She is grown up now! Will she find the right man? Will he respect her?

Melba Eldridge

This picture could represent a Church gathering of today's world.

Three out of the four people in the congregation are women.

African American Men Struggle to Seek God

Most men become a father through a biological act,

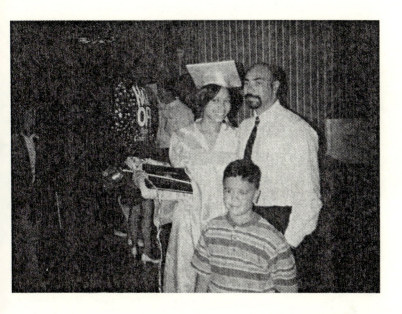

but fatherhood is not always the desire of man's heart. I am here for you now! Please tell me what to do. I am sorry I missed your growing years. I want to make it right for you.

Melba Eldridge

He will die for lack of discipline and instruction, and in the greatness of his folly he will go astray and be lost.

Proverbs 5:23 AMP

God is at the door of your heart now, knocking. Will you let Him in?

If you have never invited Jesus to be your Lord and Savior, I invite you to do so now. If you want to start over, or try to do things right this time, I invite you to do so now. If you are sorry for what happened in the past, or even ashamed of what happened in the past, I invite you to ask for forgiveness now.

If you are really feeling what is being said, you will experience a new life in Christ Jesus after this prayer.

Let us pray: Dear Father God, you are my last hope, effort and reason for living. I hear you at the door of my heart. I also heard that you love me so much that you gave your only begotten Son to die for me, for my sins that whoever believes (it is me) in Him, will not perish but have eternal life.

I also hear that I am saved by grace through faith as a gift from you, thank you.

I believe and confess with my mouth that Jesus Christ is your Son, the Savior of the world. I believe He died on the cross for me and my sins, paying the price. I believe Father that you raised Jesus from the dead (Easter) and His Holy Spirit dwells within me now. Thank you, for I am forgiven, I am saved and will spend eternity with you Father.

African American Men Struggle to Seek God

Thank you for hearing and answering my prayers. And it is in Jesus name that I pray.

Amen.

Melba Eldridge

Notes

Notes

Melba Eldridge

Notes

Notes

Melba Eldridge

Notes

African American Men Struggle to Seek God

Melba Eldridge

Order Additional Copies:

1st Books Library

2595 Vernal Pike

Bloomington, IN 47404

http://www.1stbooks.com/bookview/8856

1-800-839-8640

M. Akbar, *Chains and Images of Psychological Slavery* (Jersey City: Min Productions, 1984)

S. Carter, *The Culture of Disbelief* (New York: Harper Collins Publishers, 1993)

T. D. Jakes, *So You Call Yourself a Man?: A devotional for ordinary men with extraordinary potential* (Tulsa, Oklahoma: Albury Publishing, 1997).

B. King, *Hard Questions, Heart Answers* (New York: Broadway Books Publishers, 1996)

Melba Eldridge

King James Bible (Philadelphia: A Holman Company) – abbreviated as KJB

The Living Bible (Wheaton, Ill:) – abbreviated as TLB

        Tyndale House Publishers

Amplified Bible (Grand Rapids, Michigan) – abbreviated as AMP

        Zondervan Publishing House

J. Thibaut, H. Kelley, *The Social Psychology of Groups* (2nd ed. New Brunswick: Transaction Books, 1986).

K. Wilson, *Philadelphia Tribune*. (Online) April 2, 1999 Available: http://phila-tribune.com/040299-1-P1.htm.

T.D. Jakes' and Dr. Bernice King's books provided most of the information.

Melba Eldridge

Original Research Paper

African American Man
Struggle To Seek God

Melba L. Eldridge
April 28, 1999
African American History
HS 135, Spring 1999

African American Men Struggle to Seek God

"In contemporary American culture, the religions are more and more treated as just passing beliefs—almost as fads, older, stuffier, less liberal versions, so called New Age—rather than as the fundamental upon which the devout build their lives" (Carter, 1993, p. 14). This attitude is reflected in African American men in the late Twentieth Century who find it harder to seek God. African American men's struggle to seek God may be due to their inhibitions—childhood trauma, pride, frustration, and false expectations.

One of the inhibitors, as stated above, to African American men seeking God is childhood trauma. Childhood trauma is defined as "an emotional shock that cause lasting psychological damage" (American Heritage, 1994). Some of this psychological damage is caused by the role models that African American men choose. Often these role models are less Godly men versus Christian men per Bernice King (1996, p. 93). This choice is made "because there are too few visible black Christian men" (ibid.). For many young African American men, the only successful—success as being defined by the world versus Christianity—are athletes, drug dealers, and entertainers.

Some of these role models of young African American men provide conflicting messages which add to the problem of young

African American men seeking God. For example, Rev. Henry Lyons, National leader of the National Baptist Convention, was viewed as a man of God. But yet on February 27, 1999, was convicted of a crime against the Church (Philadelphia Tribune, 1999). There have been many other instances of role models whose actions have not reflected their messages.

The second inhibition that African American men have in the struggle to seek God is pride. Pride is "a sense of one's proper dignity or value; self-respect" (American Heritage, 1994). Pride's antithesis is submission which is the ultimate requirement to seeking God (King James Bible, James 4:7). If the African American man's pride was less valued, he would be in a better position to seek God. Seeking God gives an impression of weakness or vulnerableness according to Dr. King (1996, p. 95-96).

Pride is also an inhibitor because the African American male sees no value in the Church. His values are based on being macho and how he can "drink [his] way to sobriety, steal [his] way to wealth, and lie [his] way to justice" (King, 1996, p. 19). Their search is for respect. This respect is not found in the Church.

The third inhibition to seeking God is frustration. Frustration is a process and that process consists of "stress which turns into pressure and pressure into rage, and constant rage creates a state of weariness" (Jakes, 1997, p. 168). Some frustrations are caused by unemployment, bad relationships, no money, etc. The male is so focused on his stress that he fails to seek God. His focus is more of instant gratification than eternal salvation. This point is supported by John W. Thibaut's and Harold H. Kelley's Exchange Theory which states that:

> "People evaluate relationships through a cost-reward analysis, weighing the energy, time and money invested against the satisfaction gained "
> (1986, pp. 9-30).

The Exchange Theory explains that the cost is greater than the reward as far as time and energy spent. The energy spent leads to anxiety and frustration which decreases the African American males emotional fulfillment.

Faith, or the lack of faith, adds to the frustration of the African American man which increases his inability to seek God. "Now faith is the substance of things hoped for and the evidence of things not seen (King James Bible, Hebrews 11:1). Therefore, the African American male is seeking those things he can see (instant gratification) versus those things that he cannot (God). This leads to the conclusion that he is not focused on seeking God but on obtaining material riches.

3

Melba Eldridge

The last inhibitor, which inhibits African American men from seeking God, being discussed in this paper is false expectations. Two false expectations are racial issues and self-imposed religious requirements. The major racial issue that inhibits African American men from seeking God is religious imagery. Religious imagery is the image that one has of God and other spiritual beings. This point is supported by Na'im Akbar quote in Chains and Images of Psychological Slavery:

> For African Americans racial religious imagery is even more devastating. We have demonstrated that the one who sees himself in the Divine image is given an unnatural and a very inflated notion of what he or she is, which developed a kind of egotistical maniac. What is even worse, though, is what happen to the one who is not portrayed in the Divine imagery, and who worships a non-self in the image. In Judeo-Christian imagery, this means that the Caucasian bows down and worships himself, and the African American worships the Caucasian as a God as well" (p. 52).

(powerful quote!)

This racial inhibitor combines with the lack of submission, as discussed in the above paragraph about pride, further obstructs the African American male from seeking God.

The second false expectation which inhibits African American men from seeking God is self-imposed religious requirements. These religious requirements are termed self imposed because one places them upon oneself, but they have no religious basis. Examples of self-imposed religious requirements are: dress code, life devoid of entertainment, spiritual worthiness, other people's impression of self, and economic concerns. These and many other self-imposed requirements inhibit the African American male from seeking God.

Goldman states in The Search For God At Harvard that tribes in Africa in the Southern Hemisphere did not all convert to Christianity. Goldman's conclusion is that if all Africans in the Southern Hemisphere did not convert then not all the Twentieth-Century African American males will seek God. Four of the reasons why African American males do not seek God are childhood trauma, pride, frustration, and false expectations. Although these inhibitors exist, there is still a need for African American men to seek God because religions is "the fundamental upon which the devout build their lives" (Carter, 1993, p. 14). African American males need to seek God in their lives and be devout so they can reach their true potential.

References

Akbar, M. (1984). *Chains and images of psychological slavery*. Jersey City:New Mind Productions.

American Heritage Dictionary. (1994). Third Edition. New York:Dell Publishing.

Carter, S. (1993). *The culture of disbelief*. New York:Harper Collins Publishers.

Goldman, A. (1991). *The search for God at Harvard*. New York:Times Books/Random House Publishers.

Jakes, T. (1997). *So you call yourself a man?: A devotional for ordinary men with extraordinary potential*. Tulsa, Oklahoma:Albury Publishing.

King, B. (1996). *Hard questions, heart answers*. New York:Broadway Books Publishers.

King James Bible. Philadelphia:A. Holman Company.

Thibaut, J. and Kelley, H. (1986). *The social psychology of groups*, 2nd ed. New Brunswick:Transaction Books.

Wilson, K. (1999, April 2). *Philadelphia Tribune*. [Online.] Available:http://phila-tribune.com/040299-1-P1.htm

African American Men Struggle to Seek God

About the Author

Melba Eldridge has blended the gifts of a Nurse, Trumpet Player, Actress and Author to bring forth a bit of information on why the African-American male struggle to seek God. As a Nurse for more than twenty years she has developed a caring, compassionate ear to listen to her patients and often their family and friends as well.

As a Trumpet player she received private lessons through Goins Music Studio, Washington, D. C. She plays Trumpet in her Church Orchestra at Mt. Jezreel Baptist and also in the Takoma Park

Community Band. She and a trio of members volunteer in their Music Ministries on tours of Nursing Homes and Prisons. Another member of the Ministry reads Biblical Scriptures to the residents.

As an Actress she made her theatrical debut in two plays. Both were shown at the Public Playhouse in Landover, Maryland. The plays were "The Arranged Marriage" and "Removal 0£ the Mask". In 1986 her literary work was published in "New Voices In American Poetry"

Melba Eldridge is a graduate of the District of Columbia secondary Schools; attended the University of the District of Columbia Nursing program; graduate of the Georgetown School of Science and Arts and Montgomery College.

Let us listen to the struggle of the African American Male to seek God as the Author hears them.

Printed in the United States
915300002B